HAL•LEONARD
INSTRUMENTAL PLAY-ALONG

AUDIO ACCESS INCLUDED

CLARINET

QUEEN
UPDATED EDITION

PLAYBACK+
Speed • Pitch • Balance • Loop

To access audio visit:
www.halleonard.com/mylibrary

Enter Code
3617-4457-6106-9924

© Jorgen Angel/CTSIMAGES
Audio arrangements by Peter Deneff

ISBN 978-1-5400-3839-5

Visit Hal Leonard Online at
www.halleonard.com

Contact Us:
Hal Leonard
7777 West Bluemound Road
Milwaukee, WI 53213
Email: info@halleonard.com

In Europe contact:
Hal Leonard Europe Limited
42 Wigmore Street
Marylebone, London, W1U 2RN
Email: info@halleonardeurope.com

In Australia contact:
Hal Leonard Australia Pty. Ltd.
4 Lentara Court
Cheltenham, Victoria, 3192 Australia
Email: info@halleonard.com.au

ANOTHER ONE BITES THE DUST

CLARINET

Words and Music by
JOHN DEACON

CRAZY LITTLE THING CALLED LOVE

Clarinet

Words and Music by
FREDDIE MERCURY

BICYCLE RACE

CLARINET

Words and Music by
FREDDIE MERCURY

BOHEMIAN RHAPSODY

CLARINET

Words and Music by
FREDDIE MERCURY

Hard Rock Shuffle

Slow Rock

molto rit.

FAT BOTTOMED GIRLS

Clarinet

Words and Music by
BRIAN MAY

I WANT IT ALL

Clarinet

Words and Music by FREDDIE MERCURY,
BRIAN MAY, ROGER TAYLOR
and JOHN DEACON

DON'T STOP ME NOW

Clarinet

Words and Music by
FREDDIE MERCURY

I WANT TO BREAK FREE

CLARINET

Words and Music by
JOHN DEACON

PLAY THE GAME

Clarinet

Words and Music by
FREDDIE MERCURY

KILLER QUEEN

Clarinet

Words and Music by
FREDDIE MERCURY

RADIO GA GA

CLARINET

Words and Music by
ROGER TAYLOR

SAVE ME

CLARINET

Words and Music by
BRIAN MAY

SOMEBODY TO LOVE

Clarinet

Words and Music by
FREDDIE MERCURY

UNDER PRESSURE

Clarinet

Words and Music by FREDDIE MERCURY,
JOHN DEACON, BRIAN MAY,
ROGER TAYLOR and DAVID BOWIE

WE ARE THE CHAMPIONS

Words and Music by
FREDDIE MERCURY

CLARINET

WE WILL ROCK YOU

CLARINET

Words and Music by
BRIAN MAY

YOU'RE MY BEST FRIEND

CLARINET

Words and Music by
JOHN DEACON